unassociated tidbits and phantom thoughts

Ariel Moss

Presentation by *BookLeaf Publishing*

Web: www.bookleafpub.com

E-mail: info@bookleafpub.com

ISBN: 9789357740623

First edition 2023

This is for my grandma, my partner, my parents, and myself. Thank you for always believing in me.

ACKNOWLEDGEMENT

Thank you, Stephen, for being my soundboard and support through this journey.

PREFACE

Welcome inside my mind. I hope you find it as wonderfully terrifying as I do. If not, that's okay too. You are still invited to join the party.

A blank page.

A blank page.
Doesn't it always start that way?
Emptiness, a void—
awaiting the transcript of voice.

Waiting for the dark scribbles of thought
to just appear, to form, perfectly prescribed.
But there is no doctor here, no formula for
perfection.

It is only words and the chatter of a thousand
seconds
biting off each sentence.
It is the grey goo of the skull morphing into
dance
as fingers try to keep tempo at just a glance.

But just like that it can be gone,
forever forgotten as millisecond is yawned.

The red fringe of the sunrise

The red fringe of the sunrise
licking the horizon—
that is what gives me hope.
When the sky screams perpetual gloom,
when the brain buzz blinds me,
when the doubt of a million sighs cloud
overhead.

It is the breath of yellow that glimpses over her
that keeps my eyes waking each morning.
It is the orange peel that crashes into the blue of
a new day
that sustains the air flowing in my lungs.
It is the sun's daily salutation
that preserves life's persistent rhythm repeating
in my chest.

As I watch her rise to radiate my chilled frame,
I am reminded of summer's essence—
her radiance and my true bliss.
I am given feathers — confident soon
to bask again in her amber rays.

Dear Sunflower,

I took you for granted.
Your sweet summer scent,
cherry-kissed cheeks,
your ever-shining smile.

I thought you would be there—
leaves wrapped around me.
That you'd be there—
to meet our new family.

But the sun has hidden its face away.
The air has crisped to crackle the skin.
The sky has stolen your chlorophyll.
Your petals have cremated,
your stem has chilled,
your leaves have returned to dust.

Yet, my Earth still spins—
although, it is slant —
gaze fixed on past,
Slipping from present's grasp,
each day I forget I also remember.
I hear your buzz and relive
all of our time spent together.

Your memory shimmers in my mind
like a sienna silent film reel:
Click-click-clicking each frame to view.
Your smile— forever preserved anew.

Your blossom still brushes each butterfly,
each bumble bee,
still spreads your pollen
to each and every tree.

But the grass has still greyed,
and the leaves have still molded.
Yet the birds still chirp,
and the stream still trickles.
Breath is still breathed,
and rain is still grieved.

Goodbye, sunflower.
You will not be forgotten.
Your petals will grace my children's cheeks,
Your leaves will wrap my arms in peace,
Your roots will anchor my mind and heart.
You'll live in each meal.
You'll live in each feast.
Your presence will remain
as if it were a dandelion stain.

Muffled smiles

Muffled smiles,
smothered giggles,
back in high school,
parents' couch.

With an air of chemistry,
language of movements,
gentle brush of fingers,
we are spoken for.

Innocent play—
no unzippers,
no unbuttons—
just two mouths,
dancing to beat of day.

Interwoven hands—
laced like sneakers—
bound together to beat
cool air that stings them.

We walk side by side.
Conversation flows from
babbling brooks called mouths.

Your cool voice and assuring grip
soothe my unanswerable questions.
Your eyes are pools of understanding
that offer mine a place to wade
as we contemplate our existence.

Bodies interlock like
fingers holding palms,
life jacket arms round torsos—
pulled to safety—
breath of fresh air.

Lips hold secrets of months apart,
a luxury missed
only hours ago.
Home still found in touch,
hearts melded through tongues,
Whispered—
reminiscent breath—
osmosis in action.

Moment claimed—
just for us.
Kids again
in a skyscraper world,
young battles seem simple
as we face new.

Satisfied—we sit in silent observation

of time together.
Our bodies sing silent music—
only we can hear.
We are calm in our bubble of love,
a moment of happiness called our own.
We hold on to fantasy—
life led together—
past and future—
can it truly be...
forever?

Walt sings the body electric.

Walt sings the body electric.
He calls us to love the body—
In all of its amorphousness.
How does one love their body?
The body, a symbol of struggle—
coping with the flaws that plague it.
The body— a tool used to distance oneself from
others.
The body— holder of brain.

The brain—
Enigmatic, phantasmic, anxious, curious,
over-thinker, caller of names,
black sharpie scribbled cloud
Her fractured reflection mumbles,
"Electric who?"

Walt sings the skin.
The skin that staples together—
To keep us standing straight,
Held from melting to the floor—
As a grape popsicle
For feet to glide into its goo

The feet that keep us moving forward

Even when the rest of the body says
"Lie in bed"
"Your dreams mean nothing anyway"
"No one cares about you"

The mouth that is insatiable—
Feeding us lies that we're not good enough
While packing fat to bone
only for our resentment:
the cycle continues.

The smile that hides embarrassment,
The laughter that reduces questioning,
The eyes that lure temptation,
The hands that fidget to distract.

We are but frames that dance through the night,
celebrating another day of mediocrity.
Lips that slip us from reality,
Cleaning our souls—
Submerged in delectation.
As we burst into the universe,
We are one:
naked, reimagined, re-owned,
Beautiful, perfect, enough.
Our body:
I sing it,
Electric.

buzzing bees

Some days the buzzing bees frighten the clouds
away.
Other days the buzz isn't loud enough for the
thunder to leave.
The flora can sometimes sway their direction.

A drop of rain might help the downpour release,
but some days it feels like I'm falling with no
glimpse of light ahead while I grab for the ledge
of the pool that drowns me.

And other days it feels like I'm flying with the
sun beaming around me while I'm basking in
nature's melody.

But there are still other days when I feel like a
frog under a lily pad—
hiding from my predators while I count to ten
holding my breath not to feed them.

The funny thing is that between days is always
too short.
The length of sunshine dwindles as my heart
stops revolving around its various spindles.

Savor each moment, they say.

Okay...

maybe if I stay as still as possible time won't
lapse.
I'll be able to stay here forever.
But no.

Time keeps its slow and endless progression, the
brook retains its stream.
Hopes and yearnings thrown to dust.
I am paralyzed.

Excuses.

What a backwards way to live.
To desire infinite time
just to not use it.

I spend my smiles alone with tears to comfort
me.
My ice wears thin.
Release me.
Bees, please.
Make pain vanish,
rebirth me without pressure,
give me a life with only pleasure.

She is like the clouds.

She is like the clouds.
Her mind builds rain,
pressure gathers to grey.
Her limbs sag from their load,
darkness inflates to bloat.
Her steps slosh through life without smile,
clinging to moment that's been gone awhile.
Black scribbles blind her as
her hands grope for a reminder.
Liquid-filled visions blur compromise.
Soon, she will burst,
full of passion and rage.
Her eyes will blink thunder
while the tension meets demise.
Her lips will breathe lightning
while water spills from brain,
she will cleanse the scars of her pain.

There is magic in the coming and going

There is magic in the coming and going,
to ride the world's carousel of growing.

When the autumn browns your motivation and
the thought of grass greens your palate for
adventure, know that you must listen.

When you become blasé to sun too long sung
and crave raindrops in reflection, know that you
must listen.

When boredom greys the blank canvas of winter
to smudged slush, know that you must listen.

It is time.
It is time to go and come back.
It is time to thrive in the new and unknown.
It is time to break free from your roots,
to blow away the soil settled on your feet.
It is time to cleanse your palette.
It is time to hitch a ride on the wings of a bee.
It is time to circle every flower with hesitation
while each moment away revives another
brushstroke to color in the grey.

It is time to swipe your brush to the trees and
breathe.

But, eventually, it is time to stream through the
breeze back home.
It is time to revive your view,
to windex the grays to blues again.
It is time to pollinate your own flowers,
to settle your feet,
to reroot yourself in the beat.
It is time to snuggle in close,
as the seasons circle by,
Time's endless pirouette.

And merrily go 'round again.

Paralysis of mind

Paralysis of mind
seeps into muscle,
movement refused.
Adrift on the pond of endless rumination,
Away from the World.
Words replaced by buzz as
hives stiffen flesh to inescapable depths.
Screams of silent static,
the invisible shhh of limbs gone numb.
Ambition clings to bird's whistle,
chopped from its tree
as I stare into
the void that is me.

Hello, Sunshine.

Hello, Sunshine.
You dance on the sidewalk
with a rainbow colored scarf
flying past your face and
a tutu wafting round your waist.

You hold the simplest smile
rosy in your eyes,
sustained only by your romp.

You giggle in the light
of the cloudiest days.

You radiate the joy of
newly formed stars,
twirling fear into play.

You float past my window
like the sun and her rays.

While I watch from my garret,
breathing in memories
of days long erased.

Her rage is tectonic.

Her rage is tectonic.

Electrifying,
cataclysmic,
all-consuming.

Her eyes speak fire to the earth quaking within
as they fight to remain placid.
Her throat is stuffed with moth balls, rotting
unspoken words
Her brain becomes a rat's maze,
trying to find the cheese.
Her fists yearn to drink bricks,
to quench their thirst for blood
Her heart climbs 3 flights of stairs,
Compressing the diamond.
Her ears turn to hornets nests without pesticide
sprayers.

She has become the wind of a tornado,
the wave of a hurricane,
the magma of a volcano.
She shivers away the burst,
trying to stay tame.
She pinches her lungs to retain their heat,

which turns to shudder.
Soon, melted is the ice of her skin,
magma becomes lava,
the moon shatters in its place,
as the explosion hits their face

My mind is pressurized like a diamond

My mind is pressurized like a diamond.

It has learned to squeeze the life out of itself —
constricting its breath like a snake.
It takes all of the good ideas and turns them to
dust.
It throws the glass of its gray matter to the wall
just to see it shatter.

It says,
"fuck you,"
"You don't deserve a good time."
"I want to see you cry."

It drills at my eyes until oil is struck.
It cinches the squiggles to impossible standards.

My mind crawls to a red,
fully depleted,
and receded.
Transcended from home—
brain Pinked like the Panther.

The woman in my mind

She shines confidence: rays of shattered
illusions.
She is proud of the fat accumulated on her hips
and tits
She refuses to conform to uniformity.
She eats people's stares, absorbs them as
chlorophyll, and fuels herself on their insipidity.

She isn't afraid to say "fuck you" when
necessary.
She sure as hell isn't afraid to speak her damn
mind.
She is self-governing: dictator of her body.
She calls it her vagina, pussy, cunt, or labia.
She tells it like it is.
She speaks of sex in all of its explicitness.
She orgasms every day.

She makes all the right decisions.
She's probably vegan and does yoga all the time.
She's curvy and proud.
She can keep plants alive for longer than a
month.
She recycles and composts.
She grows a garden for her feasts.

She's ceded - washed clean of society.
She finds happiness in being unique.
She is undefined.
She revels in remaining unlabeled.
She knows what she wants and when she wants
it.
She writes her mind and works her own agenda.
She's stopped being "their's"
She is only her's.

This woman in my mind…
she is just that: a woman.
The woman that I only wish I could be.

We are alive and that is good.

We are alive and that is good.
Perhaps you are not alive and perhaps that is
also good.
They say there is beauty in life…
But is there not beauty in death as well?

Is a blue lake not more desirable than a green
one?
Are autumn leaves not awed for their courage?

The wane of a sunset that fades day into night is
not alive.
The caress of a freshly dried blanket on your
naked skin is not alive.
The warmth of a bonfire's ashes that soaks into
your clothes is not alive.
The embrace of your lover's hand is not alive.
The chirp of a bird returning to the trees
heralding spring is not alive.

Let us not forget that some of the most beautiful
things in life are not alive.
Yet we love them still.

She is alive— sprung from her cove.

She is alive— sprung from her cove.
Once huddled and warm in the comfort of home,
she has ventured out to a new unknown.
Here is where she finds it—
her true passion all on her own.
Out of her comfort zone,
stretching herself,
discovering malleability.
She is at peace here—
in her world of uncertainty.
Her craving for new breath has been sated,
her spark has been renewed—
beige moments painted blue.
Fresh eyes for a ripening horizon.
She has been resurrected from her hibernation.
She has become whole—
with a full-feathered soul.

at any moment

at any moment

intestines will fall out of mouth:
a bird with feathers plucked,
squawking down pill,
unable to seal its beak.

lips will beat with uncertainty:
a metronome composed of bone,
wandering through time to the
thump of discordant compression.

lungs will be swallowed by tongue:
a strangled snake,
unspeaking through
the viscosity of blood.

heart will release ballast, hot air balloon:
an imploded rat,
saturating the body with
its caustic juices.

brain will freeze as hail:
a clock hammered still,
exasperating at its efforts

to break the chill.

at any moment…
she could burst…
with a silent gasp
or a blaring blast.

and

just maybe

she will…

crash test dummy

I've hit a wall—
crash test dummy.
My brain has been splattered on the fractured
windshield—
visible, but just out of reach.
Letters do not come together.
Instead, they float in the ether.
My palette is full
but the canvas is blank—
vacuous and resentful.
Words climb my spine
to convince my throat they are worthy
just to be dropped from their journey.
The wheels have stopped turning,
but the engine is still rumbling,
the music still drumming.
Pen bleeds empty to vacant lines,
killing inspiration— blue blotches.
My body lies still in its broken shell
as it reminisces its existence.

I collect pebbles

I collect pebbles
And gently stack them at the base
Of the mountain that I am building.

She comes along to topple them.

I pool the pebbles back around me,
to start again.
I peel them one by one,
calling each of them to settle.

She pokes them with her finger,
anticipating her pleasure in my demise.

I paint the pebbles fruity:
green, blue, yellow, and red.
I paint the pebbles asleep:
grey, brown, white, and black.

She eats her favorite flavors,
flicking the others to the side.

I collect pebbles
and gently put them in their place.
I collect pebbles

and she laughs in my face.
I collect pebbles
and time will go on.
I collect pebbles
that will eventually be a mountain.

I crave the journey.

I crave the journey.
Each foot stepped,
Each breath breathed,
Each sound heard.

I crave the nature that surrounds me:
The feeling of life from the sun rays,
The breath of fresh air from the bird's song,
The whisper of hope from the crisp clean wind.

I crave the path that I follow,
The hills and valleys,
The climb and release
begging me to stay.

Yet I catch myself staring at the ground,
carefully stepping around leaves,
avoiding the mud,
creeping around the roots,
trudging to the end.

I forget to look up.
To admire the sunshine,
To soak in the life of a spring day.
To remember that not long ago life had ceased

and now it's back out to play.

I crave the journey,
crave the adventure of climbing for new,
never truly absorbing my time,
never happy with what grew.
Always on to the next step,
plunging towards the tape.

Daydreaming of the day it will be over only
to wish for more when it is done.
Nothing is truly good enough for me,
I am insatiable, full of craving
that will eventually eat me.
I crave the journey, but never take the time
to celebrate the moments
I have that are one of a kind.

I spend so much time looking down,
avoiding the pitfalls,
I never remember that I truly am happy.
Instead of admiring daylight's race,
I look forward to the finish line
with impatience,
leaning to break the plane,
but when I get there,
I yearn for more.

How to write a book of poetry:

Brew the coffee extra strong,
deep breath, sit with your notes app open staring
blank, start to shake,
over-caffeinated or anxious? Who's to say?

"Will you read this out loud for me?"

Ride your bike to get the blood to your brain,
type every thought, even the scary ones,
rearrange: copy/paste,
realize it's been two hours, move on.

"Will you read this out loud for me?"

Shower to release your true mind,
come up with a really good line,
reach for your phone across the room,
thank the technology gods for waterproof.

"Will you read this out loud for me?"

Reread what you just wrote,
Reread what you just wrote,
Reread what you just wrote,

Reread what you just wrote.

"Will you read this out loud for me?"

Change that one word that sounds weird,
completely dismantle your entire poem,
rewrite the best ideas, start again,
sweep up the remains, come back tomorrow.

"Will you read this out loud for me?"

Contract your partner as your unofficial editor,
spend hours contemplating semantics together,
argue the difference between word choice and
semantics, settle for semantics, move on.

Then you ask him one last time,
"Will you read this out loud for me?"

I want to say thank you

I want to say thank you
to all of those who have helped me before
in any way, shape, or form.
But I want to do it right.

I have been told I am too humdrum,
my appreciation lacks luster,
I am ungrateful and a bitch—
that I don't deserve any of this.

I promise that's not how I mean it.
it's not that I don't love it,
I just don't want to put on a show.
I want you to know that I'm genuine.

This isn't wheel of fortune.
Plastic smiles and yellow name tags
have no place here.
I want you to know, I am sincere.
I truly appreciate you and all of your support.

Inside, I am overcome by emotion that might
sell short,
so unbelievably surprised that
someone could care for me in this way,

to be so generous that I cannot repay.
I am overcome with appreciation.
My mind reminds me:
"I don't deserve this kind of love,
this kindness, or dedication."

My veins fight waves that grow in my chest,
pulling elation from eyes, but
suddenly my heart is a water park.
The bell rings, announcing the bucket full.
But I don't want you to see me cry,
even though a tempest swells inside.
You might think that I'm weak,
overly emotional, or passionate beyond belief.

So I dissociate, give all feelings to her.
She holds my tongue from speaking wrong,
she calms my tone to hush,
takes the gush of words I wish to speak
and pulls them back into a driving beat.
She cools my features, riding the squall.
She wrangles my most genuine tone,
my most appealing smile, and
squeaks out my thank you— as a loan.

We sit silently with hopes you will not see
the pleasuring pain inside of me.
We want you to know that we see you,
we see all of your efforts, all of your hard work.

We know that you didn't have to
go through all of that for us, but you did.
And our appreciation goes beyond words,
beyond actions.

So here I am.
I will away the mask,
I will push down the emotions
to give my most honest self,
I will put away the thesaurus
to stay true to words,
I will gather voice, ignore the buzz of
guilt and unworthiness eating inside,
and I will say,
thank you.

www.ingramcontent.com/pod-product-compliance
Lightning Source LLC
La Vergne TN
LVHW010925200726
843509LV00013B/2074